go

FOLLOWING JESUS TO THE ENDS OF THE EARTH

by Dave Dishman

GO

Following Jesus to the Ends of the Earth

Written by Dave Dishman

Cover Design, Rick James

Layout and Design, Will James

Editing, Christina Marty

Cru Publishing

100 Lake Hart Drive, 2500

Orlando, FL 32832-0100

ISBN –1-57334-099-5

Kesteoun muttaok Chap I. *nequtta tashikquinnu.*

NEGONNE OOSUKKUHWHONK *MOSES,*

Ne asuweetamuk

GENESIS.

About the cover: Puritan missionary, John Eliot (1604-1690), was one of the first to preach the gospel to Native Americans. In 1658, he translated the Bible into the Algonquian and it was the first Bible to be printed in North America.

The Algonquian language was difficult to speak and even more so to translate; the word for *our questions*, for example, is *kummogkodonattoottummooetiteanongannunnonmash.* Commenting on his translation labors, Eliot said that, "prayers and pain through faith in Christ Jesus will do anything."

Asked why he went to the Algonquian Indians, Eliot gave three reasons: *the glory of God*; *compassion and ardent affection* for them; and third, to accomplish *a principle end for planting the country—to communicate the gospel unto the native americans.*

In 1690 John Eliot died, age 85. His last words were "welcome joy!"

thank you

Let me say thanks to some friends who've helped in the writing and production of this book. First, thanks to Shawn Cramer, Paul Mayer and Andy Allan for reading the manuscript, proofing and making suggestions. I put many of your helpful ideas into print. Thank you to Rick James for listening to my initial idea for this book and for all your work on bringing the project through to completion. Thank you to my wife, Dawn, and to our kids, David, Matthew and Katherine for your encouragement and for going to the world with me. Finally, thanks to the missionary staff of Cru, all over the world, who inspire me on a daily basis.

Most sincerely,
Dave Dishman
March 5, 2015

contents

Then Jesus came to them and said, "All authority in heaven and earth has been given to me. Therefore go and make disciples of all nations, baptizing them in the name of the Father and of the Son and of the Holy Spirit, and teaching them to obey everything I have commanded you. And surely I am with you always, to the very end of the age." —Matthew 18:18-20

"But you will receive power when the Holy Spirit comes on you; and you will be my witnesses in Jerusalem, and in all Judea and Samaria, and to the ends of the earth." —Acts 1:8

Dave Dishman

go

following Jesus to the ends of the earth...

Preface

Boredom - my one great fear in life. Living a carefully managed existence and staying close to shore sounds like a slow shuffle towards the old folk's home. A remarkable world exists that the Lord has put before us and I've always wanted to experience it. In fact, the promise of adventure drew me across the ocean on my first mission trip. I spent six weeks of my summer in communist Romania, behind the "Iron Curtain." It sounded like a mountainous challenge, but I wanted in. I signed up, trusted the Lord for the money and got on the plane. Going on that trip remains one of the best decisions I've ever made.

Early in the summer I was asked to wait at a train station near the Black Sea in order to pick up some evangelistic materials for distribution. Because Romania was communist at the time, this was technically illegal. Or just plain illegal, technical or not. It sounded exciting, but as I sat all day at this country station, in the middle of a cornfield, the allure started to wear off. I waited from early morning until dusk for the people with the materials to show. When they didn't, I had to find my way back to our campsite in the dark, hiking and hopping trains and chasing buses. After a couple of days of waiting with the same results,

I was fed up.

No one had arrived and I felt that my time in the mission field was wasting away. While my friends were meeting Romanian students and discussing the love of Jesus, I was dozing in the shade with no one to talk to except a drunk guy who, on the second day, crawled over from under a tree and shared lunch.

On the third day I was lying on a bench with a book over my face when a train arrived. A quick glance up the tracks and I realized that my friends had not appeared, so I went back to sleep. A moment later someone approached and asked me a question in Romanian. From under my book I replied in a loud, frustrated voice, in English, "I don't speak Romanian!" Remember, I'm a missionary at this point. The young man who had approached me then said, "Oh, you speak English, may I talk with you?"

Being somewhat perceptive, I sat up and we introduced ourselves. He was a soldier who had gotten off the train for a break and was looking for a light. I had some matches, so he lit his cigarette and we began to talk. He happened to be a university student serving his compulsory military service, which was common at the time. Even though he had never spoken with a native English-speaker, his language skills were excellent. He asked if I had something to read, and in my pack I had a booklet that outlined the gospel. I pulled it out and he started reading it out loud.

After the first point—God loves you and offers a wonderful plan for your life—his hand began to quiver. He read about sin and separation from God and we talked about this a bit. When he read that Jesus is God's only provision for man's sin, he put the cigarette down because his hands were shaking too much to hold it. He kept repeating, *"I've never heard this before, I've never heard this before."* Just when he read that we must personally receive Jesus as Savior and Lord and we started to discuss how to do that, the whistle for the train blew. Soldiers all around us started scurrying to get back onboard.

As he got up to leave, he asked if he could keep the booklet, saying that he wanted to make that decision to follow Jesus. The last glimpse I got of him was through the window of the train where he was intently studying the booklet. The train pulled away while I sat stunned on the bench. It was a fifteen-minute encounter and the deepest spiritual conversation I had that summer. For some reason that God only knows, He chose to take a college student 5,500 miles from Missouri to meet another college student at a desolate train station in a corner of Eastern Europe for a short conversation, a conversation that could change everything. God will do what God will do. His economy is different from ours. God wants people to hear the good news and he will use all sorts of people and circumstances to ensure that happens.

As I've been involved in going to the world for years now, I've met fantastic people, seen wonderful sights, been nervous many times, hungry a lot, tired, surprised, shocked, frustrated, angry and lost more than once. In fact, later that same night in Romania, I was lost in the middle of a field with a pack of dogs barking nearby. I wondered if they were hungry and whether I smelled good to them. Had God used me and now it was time for my demise? Thankfully, not. Still, in the midst of all these experiences, have I been bored? No, not really. Adventure and boredom don't mix.

Aiming for the ends of the earth is an adventure, an adventure where God will use you as you step out and go. This is a lesson I've learned over thirty exciting years, both sending thousands of people to the world and going myself. Time and again I hear about lives that have been changed among the people who finally understand the truth about Jesus and among those who go and do the explaining. My hope is that through these following reflections you will catch the vision I caught years ago to follow Jesus to the ends of the earth.

When Jesus Said Go...

Two thousand years ago, a dozen or so men and women gathered on a hillside outside of the walls of ancient Jerusalem, waiting pensively under the bright sun. Assembled from a smattering of backgrounds, these were the most committed followers of Jesus of Nazareth, and they'd come to this lonely spot to hear him teach.

For several weeks they had witnessed a series of events unparalleled in human history. These were actions that would have been beyond belief if these disciples hadn't experienced it themselves, as Jesus was dead on a cross only forty days before. But since that time they saw him alive and spoke to him and touched him. One even stuck his hand into the wound on Jesus' side. Jesus ate with them and reassured them. It had been a joyous, miraculous celebration of Jesus. However, he stressed that he wouldn't stay with them forever and as it turned out, this was the last time that he spent with his most faithful disciples.

So, before he left for good, what did Jesus tell these devoted followers? What instructions did he place before them? How did he encourage them to carry on? His directions were quite simple, really. But like all that Jesus taught, in his simplicity lies a depth of profound meaning.

Jesus told his disciples to ***GO.*** He told them to make more disciples, disciples from all nations (Matthew 28). He let them know that his vision is not just local, but it encompasses Jerusalem, Judea, Samaria and the ***ends of the earth***.

Picture it. A handful of his followers, mostly uneducated, certainly not powerful or wealthy or well connected, sitting on a hill in a subjugated country at the edge of the Roman Empire. Jesus gives them an audacious goal, a great commission that will consume their lives. Jesus tells them to go and make disciples of all the nations. So what do they do? They ***go...***

Going involves a serious call

When Jesus told his disciples to go, they took him seriously. They went. They left their homes and communities and took the message out. They left to make disciples of all nations.

Those of us who follow Jesus today are beneficiaries of these first disciples. We owe them a debt. They set the tone for Jesus' disciples over the centuries. To follow Jesus involves going. It involves helping others become his disciples. Christianity is, at its core, a missionary religion. It's spread by the followers of Jesus going either next door or to the next continent to make disciples.

Followers of Jesus have embraced this teaching over the centuries. Paul, the first century apostle, was one of the greatest to go. He traveled all over the Roman Empire spreading the news about Jesus. In fact, open up almost any Bible (an archaic, printed Bible, not an app) and in the back you'll find a section of maps. One of those maps will be labeled something like, "the missionary journeys of Paul." He was a big deal.

About 400 years later, on an island far to the north, Irish raiders kidnapped a young English boy named Patricius and held him as a slave for several years. While he eventually made his escape and returned to England, something began to shift in his heart. The Lord, through visions, began to pull him once again to Ireland, this time to return as a missionary to his former captors. He sailed back to preach the gospel to the pagan Irish and eventually became Saint Patrick of Ireland, the first documented missionary outside the bounds of the Roman Empire. Patrick preached the gospel as far as he could go, "to the point beyond which there is no one," to the western edge of Ireland. Only the sea remained. He was highly determined. If Patrick had known of the Americas, I'm guessing he'd have built a boat to get there.

Fast-forward to the 1800s, when a young missionary named David Livingstone left his home in Scotland to take the gospel to Africa, a land where he witnessed "the smoke of a thousand villages, where no missionary had ever been." Soon after arriving, he was mauled by a lion, but lived to press on to share the gospel. Thanks to his pioneering work and the efforts of many others, millions of Africans are now disciples of Jesus. Their influence is broad. Some of these followers of Jesus answered the call to make disciples of all nations by going to the Xhosa tribe of South Africa.

There, a young Nelson Mandela was formed in his faith and in his ability to forgive during his years attending a Methodist grammar school. Mandela went on to become the first black President of South Africa where he stressed forgiveness and unity despite spending twenty-eight years in a prison for his political beliefs. He led South Africa through a perilous journey from apartheid towards freedom, staving off what many felt would be a time of mass bloodshed and loss of life. Why? Because he applied the teachings of Jesus that had infiltrated his young life to the political situation in South Africa. He heard those teachings because someone took seriously Jesus' word to ***go***.

How about you? Do you take those words seriously? Where should you go? You never know, perhaps there is a young Mandela in your path, just down the road, ready for the words of Jesus, ready to change the world.

Go means – don't stay!

If you look up the word go in the dictionary, you'll find a variety of definitions along the same theme. My Webster's dictionary, which I received as a high school graduation gift many, many years ago (when English was still fairly new) defines the word like this: *1) to move on a course; proceed 2) to move out or away from a place.*

As you can see, these definitions involve movement of some kind. When Jesus tells his disciples to go, he means for them to get up and move, to proceed to the task of making disciples. It is time to leave the hillside and head to a new place, to get into motion.

Like a lot of the things that Jesus encourages us to do, such as "love your neighbor as yourself," the actual teaching is fairly easy to understand. Unfortunately, putting the teaching into practice is much more difficult. Loving your loud, annoying neighbor is more work than Jesus lets on. In the case of "go," for instance, you might ask, "where?" Jesus aims us at all the nations, but where to start first? With whom? What time? What comes first? Second?

One of the glories of going in this way is that Jesus does not spell out the details. He gives quite a range of available options (all the world). He gives some direction on what you should do as you go, which is to be his witness and make disciples and love God and love others. But he leaves the place up to you. It may be far, like the outermost part of the earth (wherever that is from you) or it may be near, like across the street. But one thing is clear. You have to move to get there. You have to get off your backside and ***go***.

The ends of the earth

Isn't it interesting to think about the people who heard these words of Jesus and their world in which they lived? They heard the call to Samaria and Judea and Jerusalem and they knew those places. They lived there, walked there, slept and ate and sneezed there. They spoke the language and knew the customs. They had favorite restaurants, or at least favorite foods. It was familiar.

You have to wonder what ran through their minds when they heard "ends of the earth." The boundaries of the Roman Empire? Egypt and beyond? Persia and India? Were they afraid they'd sail off the edge of the world? They would have known little of Northern Europe and Eastern Asia and nothing of the Americas. How did they feel about the ends of the earth? How do you feel about the ends of the earth?

I'm a North American and I came to faith in a Sunday school class as a boy in Missouri. Think about this with me for a minute. When Jesus gave his commission to go, where was southern Missouri in that geographic structure? Not close to Jerusalem or Judea or Samaria. It was at the ends of the earth. Absolutely. I had the privilege of hearing and understanding the gospel in my native land and my native language because a succession of men and women took seriously the call to the ends of the earth. Missouri is about as far from that hill near Jerusalem as you can get, yet the gospel was available when my heart was ready on a hillside in Missouri.

Most of us are "ends of the earth" people. That is, we were born and raised and became followers of Jesus in a part of the world that fits into Jesus' ends-of-the-earth construct. Our faith is real to us because someone, or many someones, acted on the words of Jesus. John Calvin, the great reformer, wrote these words in his commentary on Romans:

> *The gospel does not fall like rain from the clouds, but is carried by the hands of men wherever it will go.*

Jesus says to go to the ends of the earth, to carry in your hands good news, to be his witness and to make disciples. As we've received this gospel, this gift and this teaching, it's now our turn to go. Our turn to bear the good news to whatever places the "ends of the earth" represents to us.

Disciples and Witnesses

To go means to both make disciples (Matthew 28:19):

> *Therefore go and make disciples of all nations, baptizing them in the name of the Father and of the Son and of the Holy Spirit...*

and to be witnesses (Acts 1:8):

> *But you will receive power when the Holy Spirit comes on you; and you will be my witnesses in Jerusalem, and in all Judea and Samaria, and to the ends of the earth.*

The first passage, recorded by the apostle Matthew, and the second passage, penned by the physician Luke, lays out clear directions for going to the world. The passage in Acts emphasizes being a witness, which involves telling someone what you've seen and heard. Matthew directs us to the priority of making disciples, which includes baptizing and teaching new followers of Jesus.

These are not separate or mutually exclusive activities, but rather, they represent two sides of the same coin. You might also think of it as a progression. When meeting someone new and talking about Jesus, you are first a witness to what you've seen and heard and experienced. Then, as people are interested in the message, you begin to teach and instruct them in the ways of Jesus' followers. As these new disciples embrace the faith you help them identify with Jesus. You help the young of faith grow deeper and develop more fully.

Two sides of the same coin. On the one side, going

means that you talk about, promote, discuss, or chat over (either loudly or in a whisper or through the written word) the person of Jesus. As you go, you are witnesses for Jesus. Jesus is crystal clear when he says, "you will be my witnesses." Those who go are involved in lots of good things, but always in the name of Jesus.

Mother Teresa of Calcutta ministered to the poorest of the world's poor among the Hindus and Muslims of India. She and the women of her religious order, the Missionaries of Charity, worked with men, women and children who lived and died in the streets, some literally calling holes in the ground their homes. The Missionaries of Charity were among the few Jesus followers in a city teeming with millions of adherents of other faiths. Mother Teresa was eventually awarded the Nobel Peace Prize in 1979 for her work among the poor. Throughout her life, amidst all the challenges and accolades, she always offered her services "in the name of Jesus."

On the other side of the coin, you go with a plan to help the newest followers of Jesus grow in their faith. You go with the knowledge that it will take time and work and energy to teach people to obey everything Jesus has commanded. It's not a one-and-done proposition.

Jesus tells us that the foremost commandments are to *Love the Lord your God with all you heart, mind, soul and strength and to love your neighbor as yourself.* That's quite a teaching to drop on someone who's new to the Christian faith and then leave them by themselves to ponder. This is quite a teaching for all of us to wrestle with on a daily basis. We have to help new followers of Jesus understand the depth and breadth of what Jesus was saying and we have to help them apply it to their lives. We have to make disciples. This is the hope of the world.

Both sides of the coin. Just as it's impossible to just spend one side of a coin and keep the other half in your pocket, it's also impossible to be true to Jesus' words without speaking to what you've experienced and teaching people to be true followers of Jesus.

Ambassadors

Let's go a little farther with this idea of serving as a witness. As we discussed earlier, in Acts 1:8 Jesus tells his followers to be his witnesses in Jerusalem, Judea, Samaria and to the ends of the earth. What does it specifically mean to be a witness? Again to my trusty Webster's dictionary: Witness: *1. An attesting of a fact, statement, etc.; evidence; testimony 2. A person who saw, or gave a firsthand account of, something.*

When you go as a witness, you go as a person who can give a firsthand account of how Jesus has influenced your life. You give evidence to this fact. You share your honest and heartfelt beliefs. You can give, as no one else can, the personal story of how God intersected and changed your life. It is always a powerful accounting to hear how God has reached into a person's life and brought hope.

Another word picture often used for this role is that of an ambassador. In fact, Paul the Apostle describes Jesus followers as "ambassadors for Christ." The idea of our being an ambassador brings depth and clarity to our role as witnesses. An ambassador testifies to what she has seen or heard. An ambassador is trained to communicate that message with grace and tact, even if it is a new or surprising or unwelcomed message.

Three words come to mind when I think of an ambassador: *listen, observe and respect.*

An ambassador *listens.* A good ambassador doesn't just listen to make her next point, but listens in order to understand. Good listening communicates care for a person. Isn't that why we're having the conversation about Jesus in the first place?

A good ambassador is also a careful *observer* of the people and culture around her. An ambassador is, by definition, in a place far from home. She needs to observe and learn all she can about this new culture in order to clearly communicate her message.

Then there's *respect.* Every people and culture and person you meet is worthy of our respect—at least initially. Every person you meet is a creature made in the image of God, fashioned by the hands of the Creator. To adequately convey the love of Christ to them you must convey your respect for them. How long does this take? It may take one conversation or several, but it must happen.

It's a really, really big deal to be appointed as an ambassador from your country. It's one of the most sought-after posts in the world. When Paul describes our role as an ambassador for Christ, he means it in the full weight of the word. You are representing the loving God as you go to the world. God has entrusted to you his message of hope and forgiveness. Listen to, observe, and respect those you meet, and you will find many people interested in the message you carry—the message about Jesus.

Making disciples, nothing else

Going means to make disciples of all nations. These disciples become followers, or pupils, of Jesus. We are to help them to identify with Jesus and we are to teach them the things that Jesus taught. We are to help people see Jesus clearly and to follow him fully. As you can see, the point of all this is Jesus.

Most everyone who goes, does so with this in mind. However, a curious reality often creeps in. As we go, we carry our cultural biases with us. For instance, we may be used to eating dinner at 6 pm. That's how we've always done it. That's when our parents ate dinner and that's when their parents ate dinner. That's when civilized people eat dinner. Dinnertime is 6 o'clock.

But then we cross the ocean to go make disciples in those far-flung nations and we find that they eat dinner at 9 pm. At first this is surprising and novel. We even think it's sort of cool. However, after several days of growing hungry at 6 o'clock, but being forced to wait until 9 o'clock for dinner, this practice gets annoying. You start to believe it to be ridiculous and unhealthy. You begin to say things like, "Why, their children stay up too late and they all eat too much before going to bed; as a result they don't rise early enough to get a start on the day. This is bad for their digestion, and it is even worse for their society and

Jesus can't be happy with this!" You return to your practice of dinner at 6 pm and you start to look for others you can convert to your cause.

You've arrived on their shores to make disciples of Jesus but you're now spending most of your thoughts and emotional energy on making disciples of 6 pm dinner. While it's a silly example, I've known people who've struggled with this exact thing when in another culture. Oddly, I am always starving by 7:30…

The problem lies in making other ideas besides Jesus the focus of our witness. While our focus might actually be on dinnertime, it's more likely to be our political persuasion or our economic model or our work ethic. In the past, missionaries have been hung up on getting native peoples to dress like Europeans or even to have sex in the proper way (where do you think the term "missionary position" comes from?). Jesus tells us to make disciples who will follow HIM. This is our focus.

Then, as these new disciples learn to follow Jesus and his teachings, as their mentors, we must trust their decisions on politics and morality and family and economics and yes, even dinnertime. Such critical decisions involve issues that followers of Jesus everywhere must wrestle with before the Lord and with each other. Decisions made in light of their conscience and their newfound faith will stand the test of time. Our role is simply to go and help people discover and follow Jesus. Then we learn to trust them as they do so.

We go in power

*You will receive power when the Holy Spirit comes upon you; and you will be my witnesses...*You don't go alone. This promise of the coming Holy Spirit recorded in Acts chapter 1 is fulfilled in dramatic fashion soon thereafter in Acts chapter 2, at what we now call Pentecost.

There is a source of power for those who go, power abundant and never ending. This is an incredible promise. Let it soak in for a minute. God the Father, God the Son, God the Holy Spirit. Three in one. God dwells within you and God goes with you. Afraid of what may lie ahead? That's natural, but remember that the all-powerful God dwells in you as you go. Intimidated by the people you will meet? God, who knit each of those people together in the womb, who knows every hair on their head, goes with you. Worried about visiting a land where nobody appears to follow Jesus? Remember that *the earth is the Lord's and all it contains* (Psalm 24:1). The rightful owner, the Master, the King of all lands and countries and seas and presidents and emirs and dictators and czars and queens travels with you.

Of course, none of these places is new to the Lord. He's been there all along. People have just lost him along the way, and you're there to help them rediscover him. Through every bit of this discovery process, the Holy Spirit is available and involved.

This reality brings so many interesting questions to my mind. Like, why is it hard for me to learn another language when the Holy Spirit, who speaks all languages, lives inside me? How about a little help? Also, why can't I teleport from one location to another like Phillip appears to do in Acts chapter 8? How cool would that be? Most crucial of all, is it possible to find a decent cup of coffee anywhere in this country? I wish I knew. But this point is clear—the Holy Spirit is the key to this whole enterprise.

When you ask people to become disciples of Jesus, you're not asking a small thing. Rather, you're asking something massive. You're asking for a change in their entire reason for living. This decision will change their life, their family, their future. One decision changes everything. You and I cannot change a person in this way. But the Holy Spirit can and the Holy Spirit does *all the time.* As we go, our success does not depend on us, but it depends upon our reliance on the person and the work of the Holy Spirit.

Going means adventure

Anytime you leave the familiar to step into the unknown, it's an adventure. It's a tiny adventure when you go to a restaurant in town and order a dish you've never tried before. It's a whopping adventure when you travel several time zones away and every meal for a month involves eating things you don't even recognize. Know this: when Jesus uses the phrase, *"ends of the earth"* to describe where he wants his disciples to go, he's bringing you and me into an adventure.

Will everything be safe when we go as Jesus asks us to go? Doubtful. The life of a disciple of Jesus is not meant to be safe. It is, however, meant to be fulfilling. It also happens to be exciting. It will involve hard work and you will be tired and hungry and sick of weird food and frustrated with others. That's how people on an adventure live.

If you think that you'd rather play it safe and stay home, remember the story of the man in Florida who was lying in bed when a huge sinkhole opened up under his house and swallowed him whole, never to be found again. This really happened—look it up. What's safer than lying in your own bed? The moral of this story is that if you're going to get swallowed up by a sinkhole, you might as well be out trying to do something valuable when it happens.

Adventure certainly means doing things like visiting temples in India, or riding in a taxi going way too fast in Poland, or eating scorpions on a stick in China (in case you're wondering, they're crunchy, like old popcorn kernels). But adventure also involves expanding your humanity. As you go to the world, your thought processes shift, your mindset changes and your compassion blooms. You nourish your soul. That's worthwhile. Follow Jesus to the farthest horizon and you will never be the same. That's adventurous. Ready?

People need Jesus—not religion

People are interested and responsive when presented with a great story of a person, a living dynamic person; in this case, it is the person of Christ. Going to the world means talking about this person of Jesus Christ. He is alive and real and active. People need Jesus. He is relevant today, just as relevant as 2,000 years ago or 1,000 years ago or 50 years ago.

What people don't need is more religion. In the past I heard Dr. Bill Bright, the founder of Cru (formerly Campus Crusade for Christ) and one of the great missionary statesmen of our age, say many times that religion is man's best efforts to find God through his own works. Great harm has come to people through religion over the centuries: the Crusades of the Middle Ages, the caste system in India (a few people are born into a good life while the masses suffer), and fanatical Islamist terrorism. Religion drives people to do things, often terrible things, in order to find favor with their distorted view of God. Religion is a cruel taskmaster.

In contrast, Jesus says, *my yoke is easy; my burden is light* (Matthew 11:30). Jesus brings life. Jesus brings value to every living person, wealthy or poor, educated or illiterate, kind or even cruel. Everyone is made in the image of God and deserves to know the Creator.

As we go, we go in the name of Jesus. We go as students of Jesus. We witness to the work of Jesus. We talk about Jesus' influence in our lives. We instruct people in the ways of Jesus. We baptize people in the name of Jesus. We go under the authority of Jesus and in the presence of Jesus.

Getting the picture? It's all about Jesus.

Go together

It's interesting that Jesus spoke these directions about going to the ends of the earth to a crowd of people rather than to an individual. While there is no rule requiring us to go as a group rather than going one by one, the practice over the centuries has certainly tended towards going with others. A quick glance at the book of Acts, the story of the early spread of the Christian faith, confirms this view. We first notice the church growing together in community in Jerusalem. After the church is scattered due to persecution, we begin to see missionaries traveling in groups. This was probably due to safety in travel as much as a strategic decision, but it remained the norm.

The disciples Peter and John traveled together and later Paul and Barnabus did as well. Phillip is instructed by an angel to meet the Ethiopian eunuch (if the word "eunuch" is new to you, look it up for a nice surprise) on the road and he went alone, but this is an exception. As angels tend to bring exceptional messages, I'm sure you'll pay attention if you meet one. Paul travels with Silas and stays with like-minded people wherever he goes. Paul also mentions his posse, those who traveled with him, at the end of several of his letters (see Colossians 4 for a good example).

Going together seems to be the norm. Why is this a good thing? Let me share several fabulous reasons. One, companionship along the way. Taking the message is hard work and often discouraging. You need like-minded people around you for encouragement, accountability and motivation. Two, different people bring diverse skills and abilities to any group. You don't have to be good at everything when your teammate is around. Three, you can share the load. A good team spreads the work and the emotional and spiritual burdens of going to new places. Four, physical safety is a concern in every area of the world. You are simply safer as part of a group than alone. Five, in a group you can laugh together, cry together, bitch and moan together, try new foods together and celebrate together. A party is a lot more fun when you're not alone!

Finally, to add a theological flair, we know that God exists in the form of the Trinity—Father, Son and Holy Spirit. One God in three persons, existing in relationship from eternity past to eternity future. We are created in God's image and therefore created for relationships. So, grab a group of your friends, pick a place in the world, and go!

Overcoming fears

Going to follow a call can be fearful. Going to a new place with a new message often brings doubts to mind. Apprehensions and concerns emerge. Jesus seemed to anticipate these fears at the end of his call to make disciples the world over with this astounding promise; surely I am with you always, even to the very end of the age (Matthew 28:20). When you're worried or you're frightened, remember that Jesus is with you. That's a promise unlike any you will ever receive again.

Fears about going somewhere new run a gamut. What will it be like there? Will it be safe? Will I like the food? Will it smell weird? Will I make friends? Will I be lonely? Can I find a good burger? But fears aren't limited to the places you could go. Fears exist closer to home. What will my friends think? My family? How will this affect my job? My career? What about school or my plans for my life? Where will I get the money to go? Can I trust the Lord to take care of everything here—friends, family, job, school, career, life—as I go there? Or am I too afraid to give it a go?

It takes faith to move forward when you're afraid, faith in the Lord and in his promises. Faith that Jesus really is with you as you go. By stepping out, you're putting feet to your faith. But faith is not the absence of fear. Faith is demonstrated as we move forward in spite of our fears. Faith means going to the world with fear as one companion and Jesus as the other. There will always be fears, but better yet, there will always be Jesus.

A final thought about dealing with fear. One thing that I've realized over the years is that *action conquers fear*. This is true in every realm of life. When facing fears, step forward and act. You'll feel better and gain confidence as you do so. Jesus says to go. He did not say to wait awhile and be careful and work through your reservations. He tells us to take action. Step forward. ***Go.*** Go to the ends of the earth knowing that Jesus, the Creator and Lord of the universe, walks with you every step of the way.

Don't wait!

The time to go is now. There is no better time. In many ways, there's been no better time in history. Travel is easier than ever, even if airline seats are smaller than ever. With a few notable exceptions, the world is open like never before. Communication is unmatched. Find yourself in Africa and need to touch base with someone in Europe? No problem, you can email, phone, text, video call or chat online. You can even send a letter the old-fashioned way. Lost in a city? Relax, just get on your smartphone and download a map. Want to share a passage of scripture with an interested person but cannot carry a Bible? No worries, just show them the text, in their own language, on your phone. You can even watch a clip from the Jesus Film or download any number of resources.

If we look back one hundred years ago, we'll see another golden age of going to the world. Thousands of young men and women from Europe and the United States, members of the Student Volunteer Movement, fanned out across Africa, India, South America and Asia. They talked about their faith, they built schools and hospitals, and they made disciples and taught them the ways of Jesus. Student volunteers went to the ends of the earth. Then, in 1914, this era slammed to a close.

Starting with the assassination of an archduke in Sarajevo, World War I blossomed and bore bitter fruit for the nations of the world. There were no more men to go to the mission field as they were sent instead to the battlefields of Europe. America was pulled into the war. Money, trade and travel all dried up. Millions died. Unfortunately, the end of World War I did not mark a reengagement with global missions. The worst flu epidemic ever recorded swept around the globe during 1918-1919, killing millions more. The end of the 1920s saw the emergence of the Great Depression with bread lines and desperate days. This allowed for the continued expansion of totalitarianism in Europe which had started earlier with Communism in Russia and now brought National Socialism (or Nazism) in Germany to the fore. Hitler and Stalin rose to power, plunging the world into war again in 1939.

Following World War II, much of Eastern Europe and soon China lie under communist leadership, officially atheist and opposed to any religion at all. Doors closed to missionary efforts. One half of the world's population lived under totalitarian regimes actively working to remove all vestiges of the Christian faith from their lands and history. Despite these efforts, a few brave and faithful believers served the Lord devotedly, sometimes to the death, under these governments. However, it wasn't until the 1990s that most of these countries were officially reopened to the spread of the good news of Jesus.

The state of global missions looked so promising at the dawn of 1914. As the year ended, no one knew that it would be another seventy-five years before a time matching such promise would return. Today we live in a fresh era of open borders and ease of access. How long might it last? Hopefully for years and years. But history teaches us that it won't last forever. A series of unforeseen events will spark change and all will be different. A window will close and missionary activity will cease. As Jesus said, *night is coming when no one can work* (John 9:4). Fortunately, it is still day. The time to go is now.

All nations

When Jesus tells us in Matthew 28:19 to *go and make disciples of all nations*, he had more in mind than the current, 21st century geopolitical reality. The word "nation" doesn't only refer to a country like France or Peru, but it also refers to all the distinct people groups around the world. India, for instance, is one nation comprised of hundreds (maybe thousands?) of diverse people groups, many of who speak their own language. We can't simply make one individual disciple in India and call it finished, like "we've got a disciple in India, so now on to Sri Lanka!" Rather, the call is to make disciples of every people group in India, every people group in Europe, every people group in Asia. It is a mammoth task, but it is one that is possible, especially with today's technology and ease of travel—not to mention the fact that God wants it to happen as well!

Even with all of the mission efforts in the past, did you know that there are still many people groups without a single known follower of Jesus? The problem is not the message or the messengers, but that these are often clusters of people who live in countries that are hard to access, primarily due to the fact that a majority of these countries are closed to overt missionary influence.

What's so interesting is that these people groups in difficult places may be in countries closed to certain nationalities, like Americans, but remain open to others, like South Africans. Maybe they live in a place where Koreans can set foot, or Chinese or Australians? Different doors are open to different people. Jesus gave the call to make disciples of all nations to people of all nations. Every follower of Jesus everywhere in the world is a recipient of his call. It's a call for the nations to reach the nations. It doesn't matter if your homeland has thousands of churches or only a few. Remember, Jesus presented this commission to a handful of followers when there was no church or mission structure in place at all. Yet he gave it and they went.

Tradition holds that Thomas the doubter (as a fellow

doubter he's my favorite disciple) traveled all the way to India and was killed there in pursuit of making disciples. Today, Indian Christians trace their roots to Thomas's obedience to the call of Jesus. There were no churches, no sending organizations, and no structure when Thomas and his fellow disciples went to the world. As they went, they shared the news about Jesus and built more disciples and developed churches. These new believers in turn sent out the next round of disciples, supplied with a broader base of support and encouragement. So it has gone over the centuries, sometimes more and sometimes less, as followers of Jesus responded to his call. Now it's your turn – how will you respond?

Don't stop!

Do you ever wonder how we'll know when the commission given by Jesus so long ago has been fulfilled? When will we be finished? Is there a time when we can high five, tie a bow on it and call it a day? Well...probably not. Not until the return of Jesus to the earth. The only clue Jesus gives regarding the finish line is when he says that the gospel will be preached to all nations and then the end will come (Matthew 24:14). This leads one to believe that when there are disciples of Jesus among every people group in the world, then the stage will be set for Jesus to return and we're done. Stick a fork in it. Finished. *Finito.* However, we haven't gotten there yet and so the game is still on.

Here's something else to consider in regards to this topic—the Christian faith in this world is only one generation deep. No one is born a follower of Jesus. At some point you have to choose your own path, even if you come from a long line of

Christians. If all the current Jesus followers were to die off and no one younger chose to take their place, then there'd be nothing left but the sweeping up. Each generation needs to hear the gospel afresh. Each generation of believers needs to make disciples of the emerging generation. This may seem obvious, but it must not be taken for granted.

Begin by thinking about your own Jerusalem or Judea (somewhere close by). While it's close to home, it's no less vital. Every follower of Jesus has people in their sphere of influence, like friends, family, neighbors, co-workers, students, teachers and on and on. Where might the Lord be creating opportunities for you to nudge one of these wonderful people in your life toward Jesus?

Lock in this thought - going means that we keep going. We don't stop. We don't stop at our Jerusalem or Judea or Samaria, important as they may be. We keep going until we see followers of Jesus among every tribe and every tongue and every nation. That's the call of Jesus – keep pressing on until you hear a trumpet blast and look up to see Jesus coming in the clouds. Then put down whatever you're doing because you won't want to miss what's coming next!

Bon Voyage!

Jesus' command to go to the ends of the earth is a command to be enjoyed! It may mean challenges, along with fears and discomforts and sleepless nights, and as you go to follow Jesus, you will undoubtedly experience hassles in travel and lousy meals. But more often, *much more often*, the going brings enjoyment to those who follow these words of Jesus. When you go, you will find that you enjoy the Lord who has sent you and who is with you along the way. Saying "yes" to something that is on the heart of the Lord always brings its own pleasures, on top of the pleasures of the work itself.

When you go, you will appreciate the places the Lord will take you. Okay, maybe not every place, but most places. The world is big and beautiful. There's no telling what will captivate your heart as you're out there. A sunrise in Africa, a star-lit night crossing the Iberian Peninsula or a fresh-brewed latte enjoyed at an outdoor café in South America—all good things come from the hand of God!

Undoubtedly, you'll enjoy the people you will meet. Some are close to the Lord while others are far from him (at the moment). All are made in the image of God and all are dearly loved by him. God wants only the best for them, for none of them to perish but for all to come to a place of repentance. God formed them in the womb and knows every hair on their head. Every person you will meet is an eternal creature, unique in all creation. You think that God enjoys the people he's created? Of course he does. And you should, as well.

It's one thing to walk down a foreign street and see only people of strange customs and confusing tongues. It's quite another to walk down that same street with the heart of Jesus, greeting people created to know God yet unaware of his existence. Your heart will expand as you go. Enjoy getting to know the people you meet because in doing so, you get to know your

God a little better. He is nothing, if not creative. As the comedian Steve Martin once marveled, "Those French, they have a different word for everything!" *Vive la différence!*

It's going to take some hard work

To answer the call to follow Jesus and go sounds simple, but it sure ain't easy. Going will involve a great deal of hard work. It's not bad work, certainly not drudgery, but it takes real effort. Why do I think so? First, if you are going somewhere far away (we're talking about the ends of the earth, remember), you'll need to find a way to pay to get there and stay there. Not many mission agencies provide all-expense paid experiences, and none will provide five-star accommodations. You will have to pay your own way or enlist sponsors who will give you the funds to go and serve. If you do find an agency that will pay your way, you'll find it's not a lucrative career. So, that's real work.

Leaving your current location can be hard work. It's hard to leave the ones you're close to, like your friends and family. It can be hard to leave a good job or comfortable living situation. It may be hard for you to travel, or to eat unfamiliar dishes, or to try to keep a strict diet and avoid certain foods. The new climate can be hard: it can be either too hot or too cold or cloudy all winter or terribly polluted, as many major cities in the developing world tend to be. You'll have to work hard to deal with such obstacles and inconveniences. But that's just the start, just what it takes to get going.

You will work really, really hard when it comes to

making disciples, preparing to baptize them in the name of the Father and the Son and the Holy Spirit. To have multiple conversations about the reality of Jesus Christ and the truth of the gospel involves unfamiliar levels of exertion. To go again and again and again requires a new order of energy that you may not be accustomed to spending. Teaching new followers of Jesus to observe all that he's commanded is not a talk wrapped up in an afternoon seminar. It takes patience and compassion and insight.

You may need to learn a new language to do any of this effectively. You will need to study and practice and learn new skills. You will need to learn to fail and start again. That's hard work. Great teachers are made, not born, and to go to the ends of the earth and make disciples of Jesus involves, at the very least, becoming a good teacher, if not a great one.

While all of this is hard work, happily, it is also passionate work. It is work that you can throw your heart into. It is work that you can give your full attention to, it is work to which you can give your life. To do so would be a life well spent.

Risk

Of the twelve disciples of Jesus, ten died as martyrs for the faith including Peter, who, as he was being crucified, asked to be turned upside down because he didn't feel worthy to be killed in the same manner as Jesus. The Apostle Paul also died for his faith in Jesus, beheaded outside of Rome after a long imprisonment. Both Peter and Paul are believed to have been condemned to death by Nero, the Roman emperor at the time. This same

Nero reputedly lit Christians on fire atop pyres to light his garden parties and fed Christians to the lions to entertain the masses. Let's just say that not many mourned his death back in the day. Today, radical Islamists still behead Christians who refuse to recant their faith. Being a follower of Jesus and going to the world has always involved risk.

There's the obvious risk of violence, but there's also the peril of disease. Christian aid workers labor tirelessly to battle Ebola and other diseases at great risk to themselves. Many have died attempting to care for others. Every place you go brings a risk of illness or robbery or violent crimes or political upheaval or traffic accidents.

As you consider going to the world, there's also the potential risk to your career or to your financial well-being. Current or future employers may look down on you serving the Lord in this way. Delaying graduate school or putting off career plans can be risky—you're not sure how things will turn out if you go.

Your reputation will be at risk. Many people, even many good, Christ-following people, will not understand your desire to go to the ends of the earth for Jesus Christ. It's not normal, it's countercultural, and you will be misunderstood. That's uncomfortable and risky.

If you're single and desire to be married, going can feel risky. Does the Lord have someone for me? How will I find this person if I'm in a strange, distant land? If you're married, it's risky—can my marriage survive this crazy situation? Unfortunately, some do not. Will my kids be safe? Will they develop normally in a new culture that's not our own? What will happen to my family and friends whom I'm leaving behind?

Going to the world is fraught with risk. But you know what? So is staying home and playing it safe. You could get hit by a bus tomorrow, whether in Denmark or Detroit. Random events affect both good people and bad everywhere you go. The best place to put yourself is where God would have you. It may not feel safe, it may be risky, but it's a good place. All the great payoffs in life come with risk. Who better to risk for than the Lord? When better to risk than now?

Innovation

Social commentators use different phrases to describe the fact that it's easier than ever to get in touch, and stay in touch, with people around the world. "The world is flat," is one such descriptor, while others would say, "the world is smaller than ever." I've always liked the line, "it's a small world, but I wouldn't want to paint it!" Even though the world is made smaller by technology and the relative ease of travel, there still exist significant barriers to every single person having the ability to hear and understand the gospel in local tongues and cultures.

A few areas of the world still don't have access to technology like the Internet or even reliable electricity, as strange as that sounds to us. Many people have access to the infrastructure but live under a government that censors what they can see and read online (think Cuba or China). Still other regions are so hostile to outside influences and ideas that men and women are afraid to be found reading the Bible or Christian literature (think several Middle-Eastern countries).

How do we take the gospel to places like this? Honestly, while I have some ideas, I really don't know the answers. I'm not sure what's going to work. However, I do know a couple of things. First, the good Lord above wants everyone to know about himself. Second, people like you are incredibly resourceful and innovative. There is much still to be invented when it comes to missions and making Christ known among the nations. Bright and talented people must do that inventing and many are reading this book; you just need to go to work on these issues. The Lord, the author of all creation, is ready to meet those who will put their minds to such problems and trust him for solutions.

As I ponder these thoughts I'm looking at a beautiful bridge in Argentat, France, which crosses the Dordogne River. The river is broad and swiftly flowing as it rushes through Argentat. People have been living along and crossing the Dordogne for three thousand years. For most of these years people simply crossed at fords, relatively shallow places in the river, wading through the water. As you would imagine, this was treacherous for men, women, children and animals. Then, for several hundred years, ferries transported people and goods across the river. While it was much safer, people could still drown or lose their belongings in the river. Your cow could fall out of the boat. Finally, someone figured out how to build a bridge here.

The one I'm looking at was finished in 1875 and replaced an older, wooden structure. Two piers in the middle of the river, going down to bedrock, support this rugged bridge. The spans rise high above the channel for clearance in times of flood. The bridge allows cars, trucks, buses and pedestrians to cross the river with ease. Today no one in Argentat gives any worry or thought as to how they will safely cross the Dordogne River. No one tries to ford the river anymore and the ferries no longer run. The presence of the bridge changed all that. It's solid and it's safe and it's long lasting and it's taken for granted. Bridges link people and communities and cultures and nations like few structures ever devised by humans. They are truly wonderful.

In the world of missions, there are lots and lots of bridges still to be built. Tools and technologies exist, but far too many people are forced to ford a swift and dangerous river to get to the good news of Jesus. How can we build bridges so that it's safe and easy to deliver news about Jesus anywhere in the world? That's a task for dreamers and innovators and designers, and such are many of you.

Five Bridges

Bridges are innovative, helpful and life-changing. If I may borrow the metaphor again, I want to share five "bridges," or distinct ways to be involved in missions wherever you live. It would be fantastic to cross all five bridges at some point in your life. But in the meantime, attempt to cross as many as you can, even if you're unable to cross a border.

Bridge #1 – Pray

It's simple in theory yet challenging in practice. Jesus tells us that, the fields are white for harvest, therefore ask the Father to send out laborers into the harvest fields (Luke 10:2). We're to pray for laborers, people who will go and tell others the good news. You can pray for the needs of the world without ever leaving your hometown. The opportunity may never arise that allows you to go to another part of the world as an ambassador for Christ, but the opportunity already exists for you to influence such places and peoples through prayer. Prayer moves the hand of God. Why not try it right now? Pause from your reading and ask the Lord to send more workers into the harvest fields. Pray for a particular place or group of people who are on your mind. As you do so, you're crossing the bridge of prayer.

Bridge #2 – Give

Giving means to be generous of your time, talents and treasures. But let's face it, most of us find it hardest to be generous with our money. Money is power, money is security, money is prestige, money motivates and money means success. The scriptures are full of references encouraging us to give away our money. Why? Because ultimately God is power, God is security, God is prestige, God motivates and God brings success. Money replaces God in our hearts and there's not room for both. As a famous person once said, *you cannot serve both God and money* (look it up)! It's one or the other. How do we defeat the tug of money on our hearts? We give it away.

A wonderful place to practice this discipline is in missions. Almost every missionary and missions' agency is underfunded. More people would go if they just had the funding. Practice giving in a way that costs you something and that involves a sacrifice on your part. Pass on the coffee you buy every morning and give to missions. Or better yet, keep the coffee and pass instead on the doughnut you buy with the coffee and give that to missions. You'll still get the caffeine you need, you'll avoid those empty calories and you'll advance the cause of Jesus around the globe. As Michael Scott, of the television show *The Office*, says, that's a "win-win-win," something we're all after.

Now, some of you reading this will be blessed with the ability to generate vast amounts of wealth during your lifetime and may have the ability to give millions of dollars or euros to the cause of world missions. It will be a challenge, but it will be a great service to the kingdom. Others of you will need to pray for the ability to give a little when all you have is a little, which may prove to be a greater challenge. But we are, every one, asked to give and give generously all of our lives.

Bridge #3 – Learn

Curiosity is vital to missions. There's no substitute for learning about the world around you. Does one part of the map interest you more than another? Always thought it would be cool to visit Africa? Did your ancestors travel from another country to get to where you were born? Or maybe even your parents? Go online or go to the library and start learning about places that intrigue you. If no place comes to mind then ask the Lord this question, "Lord, what's an area of the world you'd like me to know more about?" Go with the first place that pops into your head.

An Internet search will provide tons of information about your places of interest. A search for recent news stories will help bring you up-to-date on the politics and needs of the people of each country. Research on religious beliefs or activities or festivals will yield new insight. Don't let the overabundance of material scare you. Skim a little, pray as you go, and ask the Lord to use what he will.

Maybe you'll get the chance to visit with people from the nation on your heart or maybe even take an excursion to the country itself. If so, don't hesitate. Do it. Nothing aids learning like hands-on experience. You will be forever changed and your heart will be captured. That's a good thing. Whether it's reading, watching videos, meeting people or travelling, learning is vital to the missionary mindset. Let your mind wander all over the world. You will not cross a bridge, let alone build one, if you have no interest or concern with what's on the other side!

Bridge #4 – Send

Sending involves building the bridge and helping others to cross it. This includes learning and giving and praying, but this especially involves encouraging. You won't find many people who will encourage you to give up your plans and go to the world as a missionary. The idea of you leaving your home and culture is foreign to most folks. Historically, people have left their homelands for two basic reasons: tragedy and opportunity. War, disease, famine and pestilence send refugees across borders in search of safer places.

The Great Famine of Ireland in the 19th century, caused by the failure of the potato crop in successive years and a callous government, sent Irish immigrants to the U.S., Canada, Australia and elsewhere. So many came to the U.S. that there are those who claim that up to 25% of all Americans have some Irish blood running through their veins. Of course, this statistic may simply be an invention of those who promote Irish pubs and Saint Patrick Day parades, but regardless, many good people were forced to flee Ireland in order to survive. The other reason people leave their homes is for opportunity. The promise of free land provided by the United States government in the 1800s drew thousands and thousands of settlers to the American West. They left homes, familiar surroundings, family, and especially problems for the dream of a new life.

Few, however, leave in order to help strangers find their way to God. Some have described sharing the good news of Jesus as, "one beggar helping another beggar find bread." We are not often encouraged to beg. A sender is one who helps others go. You can be one who speaks highly of missions and one who gives an enthusiastic response when hearing of a friend's desire to go. You can gather other like-minded people to pray for and promote missions. You can be a voice for missions in your local church. People will need your encouragement to go, and if you look, you will find many ways to help others get to the field.

Bridge #5 – Go

You cross this bridge as you head to the world or as you cross the street to talk to someone about Jesus. Everyone who's a follower of Jesus, who claims to be a disciple, should try to go at some point in life. You may not get very far and it may not mean a life-long calling to live in a new part of the world, but go, we must. Go for a week, a month, a year or a decade. Try it. Do it.

You won't regret it. Remember, adventure is worthwhile! As John R. Mott, the director of the Student Volunteer movement once observed years ago, there are many places "where open doors remain unentered."

Going to the ends of the earth, missions, and involvement in the Great Commission as given by Jesus is not an optional item for his disciples. All Christians are invited and expected to join in. It's a participatory exercise. Christianity is a missionary religion. So pray and give and learn and send and go. Cross a bridge. Let's do something together to change the world.

Be strategic

So you're taking this all seriously and you're considering where to go and what to do as you follow Jesus' instructions to go to the world, now where do you start? Should a person spin the globe, close his eyes, stick a finger on a spot and then run there willy-nilly in order to save the natives? Let's say no to that idea, although it has been done before and if you want to go that direction, well, it's your life. However, let me share a few words in support of thinking strategically. On the one hand, God could use you if you chose to run around the planet handing out gospel tracts. But on the other hand, God certainly uses those who use the mind the Good Lord gave each of us.

If you could only choose one audience to hear your message about Jesus, which audience would be the most strategic? Who has the most potential to bring change to their home countries? Who is the most receptive to hearing? Who is the most open-minded? Who will be the most influential in coming years? The answer is simple. You go to the young people of any nation or culture.

You win the young and you win the world. Which young people have the potential to be the most influential? The college and university students of the world. While this group comprises roughly 1% of the world's population, from this small slice of humanity comes almost every leader of every society around the globe. All the doctors, attorneys, engineers, teachers and almost all political leaders spend several years studying at a university. During this time students are most open to new ideas and most able to act upon them. Worldwide, students are more accessible than ever and are moving away from home, be it physically, emotionally or intellectually. Students are in the process of becoming their own persons and part of this process involves either embracing the religion of their parents or heading in a different direction.

The university student culture around the world is increasingly monolithic. Students listen to the same music and watch the same movies on the same smart phones while wearing the same headphones and dressing in the same styles in South America and China and Africa and the U.S. There are exceptions, of course, but most students feel more in common with a fellow undergraduate from another country than with their grandparents back home. This is an easy cultural bridge to cross if you're currently a university student or have ever been one.

By reaching the future leaders of a country, you are influencing them for a lifetime. You will also influence the broader culture around them as they step into positions of leadership and responsibility. Their views of the poor and downtrodden will change as Jesus changes their life. Jesus will begin to give them eyes of compassion and hearts of concern for their fellow citizens. They will notice people they've never noticed before. They will begin to love the Lord with their hearts and minds and souls and they will begin to love their neighbors. Herein lies the hope for lasting societal change.

Now, I'm not minimizing missionary efforts to every other section of society. All are important and it's most important to follow the Lord where he guides you. As we've said before, every man, woman and child is a magnificent being created in the image of our Holy God. If God has called you to another segment of humankind then blessings to you – Godspeed! God will use your efforts. The point is to go somewhere. Even willy-nilly is better than doing nothing at all!

Surrender

To *follow Jesus* is a phrase we use a lot in the religious world. To be a follower of Jesus, a disciple of his, carries several implications. One of the most obvious should be that Jesus is the leader. The disciple follows and tries to emulate the master. We are saying that Jesus is the director of our lives. We are choosing to *surrender* to Jesus. What an interesting choice of words. We usually equate surrendering with losing or failure. Maybe at one time we've been forced to surrender our rights. When you lose the war you're forced to surrender on the winner's terms. In this case, however, we're saying that we are giving control of our life to Jesus. It does involve giving up our rights to our lives. It is serious, not something to enter into lightly. When one declares that *Jesus is Lord*, that means that Jesus is the power of your life, the controlling center, the North Star, the guide, the boss, the general, the one to whom you bow your knee.

Remember how people treated Darth Vader with such fear and deference in the *Star Wars* movies? How they bowed before him as their "lord"? Well, in a weird way, it's similar with Jesus, except Jesus is about a millions times more powerful and loves you deeply (and is actually real). It's that type of power and love to which you are surrendering. Personally, I don't instinctively bow to anyone. I was raised to be self-sufficient and make my own way in the world. As a fiercely independent American I learned about how my forefathers threw off the yoke of King George III and today we kneel to no king. But Jesus is no king. Jesus is the King of kings and the Lord of lords. Jesus is the Creator of the universe and he holds all things together. All that we have comes from his hands. To Jesus, I bow. To Jesus, all will bow, either today or tomorrow or in eternity.

To go into the world, to proclaim the good news and to make disciples of Jesus, means that you must do so surrendered to Jesus. If you have not consciously, in prayer, given your life and all that's a part of it to Jesus, I suggest that you do so now. Devote some time to think and pray. Write out your thoughts, sign and date the document, and save it. When life gets difficult, when the going gets tough (to use an old cliché) you will have a reminder of the decision you've made to serve the One True King.

A young man boarded a ship about one hundred years

ago headed for China. He had been waiting and preparing and it was finally his time to go to the mission field. Henry Borden was from Chicago, a graduate of Yale University and filthy rich. In fact, he was a member of one of the richest families in America. He stood to inherit the family enterprise and fortune. His father was terribly upset, as he wanted his son to remain in Chicago and build their business. I would also guess that his father feared for his son's health and even his life, as sailing for China at that time, before antibiotics and other modern health advances, was fraught with danger. But Henry Borden had surrendered to Jesus years before.

His Lord had called him to China and so he answered the call. Family disapproval, a fantastic job, loads of money and social status could not sway him. In Egypt, on the way to China, he stopped to study at a language institute for missionaries. While there, he contracted meningitis and died suddenly at the age of twenty-three. Jesus, his Lord, who called him first to China, had now called him home.

Friends, family and fellow student volunteers were dismayed, but they didn't yet know the depth of Henry Borden's surrender. Borden's Bible was located and sent home to his family. Inside the front cover, penned by his own hand, were these three phrases by which he had chosen to live his life:

No Reserve, No Retreat, No Regret.

Henry Borden surrendered to whatever Jesus had for him, even if that meant death on the way to China. "Borden of Yale" became a rallying cry for student missionaries. What first seemed like a waste of a young, promising life motivated thousands to go into the mission field.

How about you? What would it take for you to write on the flyleaf of your Bible those same words?

No Reserve, No Retreat, No Regret.

no reserve

no retreat

no regret
your name goes here

A Quiet Word About Suffering

Let's tread lightly as we approach this topic—sneak up on it if you will. Sort of like you're approaching an elephant in your living room. It's really, really interesting, but you don't want to get stepped on. Or pooped on.

The apostle Paul, one of the first and greatest of all missionaries, left us this account about his adventures of going to the world for Jesus. Notice the suffering...

> *Are they servants of Christ? I am a better one—I am talking like a madman—with far greater labors, far more imprisonments, with countless beatings, and often near death. Five times I received at the hands of the Jews the forty lashes less one. Three times I was beaten with rods. Once I was stoned. Three times I was shipwrecked; a night and a day I was adrift at sea; on frequent journeys, in danger from rivers, danger from robbers, danger from my own people, danger from Gentiles, danger in the city, danger in the wilderness, danger at sea, danger from false brothers; in toil and hardship, through many a sleepless night, in hunger and thirst, often without food, in cold and exposure. And, apart from other things, there is the daily pressure on me of my anxiety for all the churches. Who is weak, and I am not weak? Who is made to fall, and I am not indignant?* —2 Corinthians 11:23-29

Going to the world as an emissary of Jesus means that you quite likely will suffer for it. You for sure will have sleepless nights and exhausting days. You will eat something that makes you sick and you'll fend off mosquitoes in the night. All normal, but still not pleasant. You and your message may face rejection. Some will gladly listen, but many will not. Some will oppose you face-to-face while the passive indifference of others will eat away at your enthusiasm for the Lord and his calling on your life. Finally, some will face, like Paul and countless others, physical blows and beatings. It's a sobering fact, but angry people still kill Christians in retaliation toward the message of Jesus. This happens today and yet is rarely even talked about. Honestly, most of the world won't care if it happens to you.

Most likely, however, you'll suffer the disregard and ridicule of those who don't believe in your cause and who don't understand what motivates you. It will pain you because many won't even want to know. That's actually quite normal. You are a messenger of Jesus to them as well. We do well to remember what Paul says later in the same passage:

> *For the sake of Christ, then, I am content with weaknesses, insults, hardships, persecutions, and calamities. For when I am weak, then I am strong.* —2 Corinthians 12:10

Conclusion

In Athens, Greece, one of the wonders of the ancient world, a temple called the Parthenon, sits atop the Acropolis, a fortified hill with a commanding view of the surrounding city and beyond. When visiting there you can easily see why the site was chosen for temples dedicated to various gods, including Athena, the namesake for the city of Athens. Although millions climb the steps of the Acropolis annually (I heartily recommend a visit), no one bows and prays to Athena in the Parthenon anymore. Her day, like the days of all the gods and goddesses of ancient Greece, has passed.

Just below the Acropolis, on a knob of rock where the notables of Athens once held court, many people do stop and pray. This is Mars Hill, the place the Apostle Paul delivered his famous missionary sermon as recorded on Acts 17. Here is a visionary spot to pause, look out over the city and reflect on the words and mission of Paul, and by default, the words and mission of Jesus. Paul traveled to Athens at great cost. He took an even greater risk to proclaim to a highly religious people that they were missing the One True God. It's recorded that following his insightful and well-reasoned sermon, some in the crowd sneered in disbelief. Others, however, were intrigued and wanted to discuss the ideas further with Paul. A few more became followers and believed his message about the True God who has risen from the dead. Not a bad day for a traveling evangelist.

Today in modern Athens, followers of Jesus still share the message with those who will listen. In every direction from Athens, men and women with the same heart of Paul, the same desire to clearly share the love of Jesus, do so in Africa, Europe, Asia, Australia, the Americas – everywhere. Paul's sermon is studied and his missionary practices are emulated worldwide. Not a bad legacy for the traveling evangelist.

Paul heard the call of his Savior on the road to Damascus. He chose to take the next road and then the next and go to Athens and many other cities where the gospel was desperately needed and where people were ready to meet Jesus. How about you? The call to which Paul responded, and Jesus' disciples responded, and countless more of our forbearers in the faith responded, still rings clearly for us today. It is not finished. What role will you play in going and making sure that everyone has a chance to meet Jesus?

Are you ready to ***GO****?*

What Do I Do Now?

How should you respond to the challenge to go? What are your next steps? Here are a few suggestions from my vantage point of helping many people think through these questions over the years:

1. Pray. Seek the Lord and ask, "What plans might You have for me?"

2. Plan. Refer back to the 5 Bridges section of this book (page 47). What bridge should you cross first: pray, give, learn, send or go? When should you do so? What strategies do you need to put into play to help you move forward? Whose help do you need?

3. Commit. Do two things. Write your plans down and tell someone you trust. Both actions will help you follow through when circumstances threaten to slow you down.

4. Go. Move forward in faith.

Books about missions

Here is a list of books dealing with different aspects of missions that I've enjoyed and so recommend to you.

How the Irish Saved Civilization
by Thomas Cahill

The Rise of Christianity
by Rodney Stark

The Decisive Hour of Christian Missions
by John R. Mott

Shadow of the Almighty
by Elisabeth Elliot

From Jerusalem to Irian Jaya
by Ruth Tucker

Eternity in Their Hearts
by Don Richardson

Meeting Miss Irby
by Joshua Irby

The Outrageous Promise
by David M. Robinson & Gabor Gresz

Come Help Change the World
by Bill Bright

Missionary
by Christopher Marco

When Helping Hurts
by Brian Fikkert

Let the Nations be Glad
by John Piper

The Gospel in a Pluralistic Society
by Lesslie Newbigin

A History of Christian Missions
by Stephen Neill

More about the author

First, I have a blog. Check it out and send me a note at gototheendsoftheearth.com (I know, it's a horribly long blog address). I have had the privilege of serving as a staff member with Cru for thirty years, working in a variety of leadership positions. I currently enjoy my role as the National Innovation Director for Global Missions. I'm married to my wife, Dawn, and have three adult children. I live in Colorado and I like to read, hike, play golf and travel the world.

Second, I always enjoy knowing something about the underlying beliefs of the authors that I read. In light of that, I want to share with you some of the principles that guide my life and motivate me to be involved in missions. I call this my manifesto, which is an impressive word that means a "public declaration of principles, policies or intentions."

- I am a follower of Jesus. Jesus's message is revolutionary. As I let his words guide my thoughts and desires I will be drawn to his cause.

- People need Jesus. People also need food, clean water, shelter and clothing. But people need Jesus at the most fundamental level.

- I want to help change the world. All people of goodwill sense that something is broken. I would like to be involved in fixing some of the broken things.

- People need others around them who've been changed by Jesus. Christianity at its best produces disciples who care about others, those who will rush to Haiti or Thailand or New Orleans or anywhere there's a need. It produces others who will stay and tend to the sick when Ebola ravages West Africa. I want to promote a faith that develops these types of Jesus-followers.

- Many people around the world are enslaved to flawed religions, beliefs and dogmas, while others are literally held in physical slavery. Too many in our world worship success, money and celebrity, eyes blinded by the allure of shiny things. I want to help set all people free.

- I believe that the gospel can permeate any culture. Followers of Jesus need to set the world alight with the gospel and let it burn. We are sort-of like Jesus-arsonists.

- Control is the most insidious temptation for Christian leaders and the greatest hindrance for the development of Christian movements under the direction of the Holy Spirit. The faith spreads when disciples are energized and encouraged—not controlled.

- I want to be involved in adventurous things.

- As a follower of Jesus, I run my political beliefs through a sieve of scripture and the teachings of Jesus. My politics are subservient to my faith in Jesus.

- I continue to work in the sphere of university and college students because I believe that no group is better suited to change the world. Students have the time, the resources, the enthusiasm, and the education to spread the good news. They are the future leaders of the world.

- I am a Christian environmentalist. I take the injunction to steward the earth seriously.

- The ones who've gone before us, the great cloud of witnesses, continually motivate me. Faithful Christ followers throughout history, like Patrick of Ireland, who lived and embodied the best principles of the faith.

- I continue to read the Gospels and the words of Jesus over and over again. They never cease to amaze, challenge and comfort me.

More from Dave and more about global missions at

gototheendsoftheearth.com

NOTES

NOTES

NOTES

NOTES

More ministry resources can be found at

Crupress.com

If you enjoyed GO
you may also find The Finishers,
by Roger Hershey and Jason Weimer,
a helpful resource for global missions.